TOOLS FOR CAREGIVERS

- **F&P LEVEL:** C
- **WORD COUNT:** 36
- **CURRICULUM CONNECTIONS:** sports

Skills to Teach

- **HIGH-FREQUENCY WORDS:** go, he, let's, off, on, runs, she, the, to, walks, we
- **CONTENT WORDS:** bars, beam, flips, gym, jumps, lands, mat, rings, stretch, swings
- **PUNCTUATION:** exclamation points, periods
- **WORD STUDY:** /j/, spelled g (gym); long /e/, spelled ea (beam); short /a/, spelled a (lands, mat); short /i/, spelled y (gym); short /u/, spelled u (jumps, runs)
- **TEXT TYPE:** factual description

Before Reading Activities

- Read the title and give a simple statement of the main idea.
- Have students "walk" through the book and talk about what they see in the pictures.
- Introduce new vocabulary by having students predict the first letter and locate the word in the text.
- Discuss any unfamiliar concepts that are in the text.

After Reading Activities

Show readers more images of gymnastics. Have they seen or watched any of these events before? Maybe some have tried tumbling or have walked on a balance beam. Draw a straight line on the sidewalk or form a line out of tape on the floor to mimic a balance beam. Ask readers to walk on the line without losing balance. What does it feel like?

Tadpole Books are published by Jump!, 5357 Penn Avenue South, Minneapolis, MN 55419, www.jumplibrary.com

Copyright ©2022 Jump!. International copyright reserved in all countries. No part of this book may be reproduced in any form without written permission from the publisher.

Editor: Jenna Gleisner **Designer:** Molly Ballanger

Photo Credits: iStock, cover; Anatoliy Karlyuk/Shutterstock, 1; CasarsaGuru/iStock, 3; Alexander Sorokopud/Shutterstock, 2br, 4–5 (left); MidoSemsem/Shutterstock, 4–5 (right); samards/iStock, 6; Sasha Samardzija/Shutterstock, 7; K_Lang/iStock, 2tr, 8; Thomas Barwick/Getty, 2ml, 9; Master1305/Shutterstock, 2bl, 10–11; Robert Decelis Ltd/Getty, 2tl, 12–13; Mike Kemp/Tetra Images/SuperStock, 2mr, 14–15 (foreground); Polhansen/Shutterstock, 14–15 (background); Image Source/iStock, 16.

Library of Congress Cataloging-in-Publication Data
Names: Kenan, Tessa, author.
Title: Gymnastics / by Tessa Kenan.
Description: Minneapolis, MN: Jump!, Inc., 2022. | Series: Let's play sports!
Includes index. | Audience: Ages 3–6
Identifiers: LCCN 2021016276 (print) | LCCN 2021016277 (ebook)
ISBN 9781636902616 (hardcover) | ISBN 9781636902623 (paperback) | ISBN 9781636902630 (ebook)
Subjects: LCSH: Gymnastics—Juvenile literature.
Classification: LCC GV461.3 .K46 2022 (print) | LCC GV461.3 (ebook) | DDC 796.44—dc23
LC record available at https://lccn.loc.gov/2021016276
LC ebook record available at https://lccn.loc.gov/2021016277

LET'S PLAY SPORTS!

GYMNASTICS

by Tessa Kenan

TABLE OF CONTENTS

Words to Know..............................2

Let's Go!.....................................3

Let's Review!..............................16

Index..16

tadpole books

WORDS TO KNOW

bars

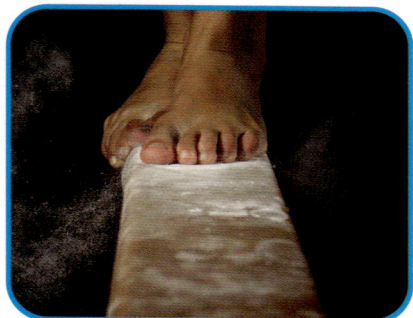
beam

flips

mat

rings

stretch

LET'S GO!

gym

Let's go to the gym!

We stretch.

She runs.

She jumps!

balance beam

She walks on the beam.

She flips!

ring

He swings on rings.

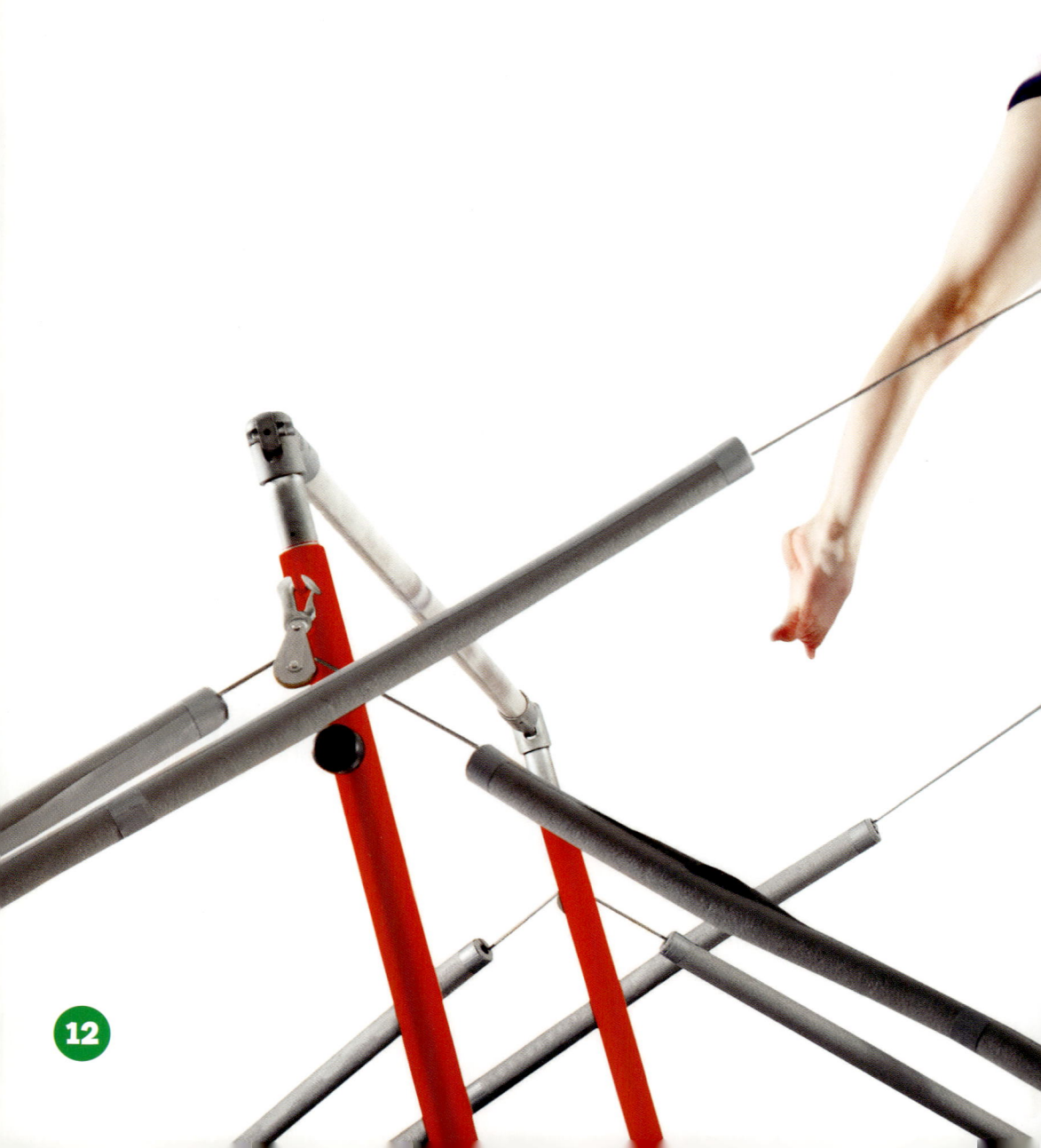

She jumps off.

mat

She lands on the mat!

15

LET'S REVIEW!

What is this gymnast doing?

INDEX

bars 13
beam 8
flips 9
jumps 7, 14

lands 15
mat 15
rings 11
swings 11, 13